Contents

AGES 7–8
KEY STAGE 2

Premier ENGLISH

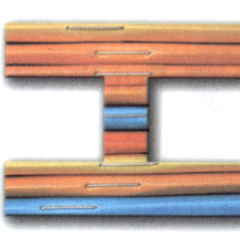

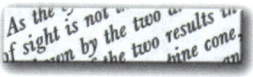

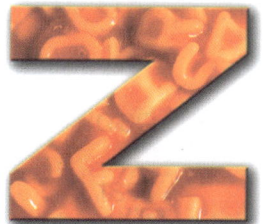

Word families

Many **words belong** to word families. Being able to spell one word in the family can help you to spell the rest.

spoon   moon   balloon

I   Put these words in their correct families. The first one has been done for you.

a light	**d** goat	**g** fright	**j** bright
b boat	**e** play	**h** tame	**k** hay
c name	**f** frame	**i** loan	**l** lay

ight

light

_____

_____

_____

oa

_____

_____

_____

_____

ame

_____

_____

_____

_____

ay

_____

_____

_____

II   Write down two more words for each of these word families.

a	stain	lain	_____ _____
b	allow	bow	_____ _____
c	plate	grate	_____ _____
d	sail	pail	_____ _____
e	book	rook	_____ _____
f	tear	near	_____ _____
g	teach	preach	_____ _____
h	spent	lent	_____ _____
i	swell	fell	_____ _____
j	hive	strive	_____ _____

Spelling verbs

When we add *ing* to a verb, we have to **take care** with spelling.

Several verbs ending in *e* (like **smile**) lose the *e* when you add *ing*.

Several verbs with a short vowel sound in the middle, like the *u* in **run**, double the final consonant.

Kate is smil**ing**.

Rob is ru**nn**ing.

I Look at each verb. Then circle its correct *ing* spelling.

a	hope	hopping	hopeing	hoping
b	bake	bakeing	baking	bakking
c	clap	claping	clapeing	clapping
d	spin	spining	spineing	spinning
e	win	wining	winning	wineing
f	lose	losing	lossing	loseing
g	shut	shuting	shuteing	shutting
h	fit	fitting	fiteing	fiting
i	make	makeing	making	makking
j	swim	swimmming	swimming	swiming
k	slip	slipping	slipeing	sliping

II Write out these verbs with their correct *ing* spelling.

a ride + ing = _____

b plan + ing = _____

c sit + ing = _____

d shop + ing = _____

e stare + ing = _____

f jog + ing = _____

g slip + ing = _____

h hate + ing = _____

i rub + ing = _____

j hit + ing = _____

k raise + ing = _____

l shake + ing = _____

Words ending in *le*, *al* and *el*

A **common spelling pattern** we need to learn is *le*.

bottle

candle

Other spelling patterns that sound the same are *al* and *el*.

medal

angel

I Do these words end with *le*, *al* or *el*? Choose the correct ending. Then write out the whole word.

a app + __le__ = ___apple___

b met + _____ = _____

c parc + _____ = _____

d chann + _____ = _____

e doub + _____ = _____

f ripp + _____ = _____

g lab + _____ = _____

h ped + _____ = _____

i cannib + _____ = _____

j pudd + _____ = _____

II The bold word in each sentence has the wrong *le*, *al* or *el* ending. Write the word again at the end of the sentence, making sure you use the correct ending.

a I am building a **modal** aeroplane. _____

b Mum put the **kettal** on to make a cup of tea. _____

c Dad took me to the **medicle** centre when I was ill. _____

d I love riding my **bicycal**. _____

e I had to dance in front of a **panle** of judges. _____

f We are going to **traval** to France by coach. _____

g My **littel** brother is only three years old. _____

h We sat at the **tabal** to do our homework. _____

Prefixes

You can add prefixes to the **beginning** of some words to change their meanings.

happy

<u>un</u>happy

Different prefixes mean different things.

un = not   dis = not   re = again   pre = before

I Choose *un* or *dis* to make these words mean the opposite. Then write out the new words.

a ___un___ + able   =   ___unable___   f _____ + popular = _____

b _____ + seen   =   _____   g _____ + do   = _____

c _____ + qualify   =   _____   h _____ + appear   = _____

d _____ + usual   =   _____   i _____ + own   = _____

e _____ + obey   =   _____   j _____ + tidy   = _____

II Choose the correct prefix *un*, *dis*, *re* or *pre* that fits and write the completed word in the correct list.

a _____well   d _____pare   g _____agree   j _____lucky

b _____cycle   e _____turn   h _____honest   k _____build

c _____allow   f _____kind   i _____dict   l _____vious

un (not)

_____

_____

_____

_____

dis (not)

_____

_____

_____

_____

re (again)

_____

_____

_____

_____

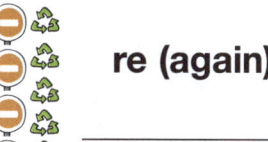
pre (before)

_____

_____

_____

_____

Synonyms

Synonyms are words that have **similar meanings**.

fast

speedy

quick

Choosing synonyms for words we use a lot can make our writing more interesting.

I **Write down two synonyms from the box for each word.**

> glum   pleased   huge   tiny   unhappy   freezing   small   excellent
>
> after   joyful   brilliant   large   chilly   unkind   mean   later

a big   _____ _____   g sad   _____ _____

b little   _____ _____   h happy   _____ _____

c good   _____ _____

d cold   _____ _____

e nasty   _____ _____

f then   _____ _____

II **Write down a synonym for each of these words.**

a run   _____   g fast   _____

b laugh   _____   h old   _____

c wet   _____   i walk   _____

d hungry _____   j closed   _____

e speak   _____   k begin   _____

f seat   _____   l simple   _____

6

Speech marks

Speech marks show that someone is **speaking**. We write what the person says between the speech marks.

'Today is my birthday,' said Jack.
Molly said, 'Happy birthday.'

I Add speech marks at the end of the speech in these sentences. Take care to put them the right side of the comma. Use the examples above to help you.

a 'My best friend is Max, said Joel.

b 'I love football, said Rita.

c 'We are going swimming today, said Mum.

d Martin said, 'That is my bag.

e 'I have a new puppy, said Alfie.

f The teacher said, 'It is raining today.

g Dad shouted, 'Do not forget your coat!

h 'Let us watch TV, said Sophie.

II Look carefully at where the speech is in these sentences. Then add the speech marks.

a I am going skating tomorrow, said Heather.

b Sarah said, That is not fair!

c Harry sighed, I love chocolate cake!

d I would like a drink please, said Lucy.

e Look at my new bike, said Katy.

f The bus driver called out, This is your stop!

g Time to tidy up, shouted Mrs Moors.

h Gran said, See you soon!

Verbs

Verbs tell us what a person or thing is **doing**.

A fish **swims**.

Choosing the right verb can also tell the reader exactly how a person or thing does something.

This frog **hops**.

This frog **leaps**.

I Underline the verb in each sentence.

a The sun shines.

b Birds fly.

c Molly reads a book.

d Sam paints a picture.

e Chris watches television.

f Matthew waits for the train.

g Charlotte munches her lunch.

h The lorries turn a corner.

i He shut the door.

j The school bell rings.

II Write the verbs in the box next to the verb with similar meanings.

dash	slumber	see	build	peer	sprint
watch	jog	snooze	create	doze	assemble

run _____ _____ _____

make _____ _____ _____

sleep _____ _____ _____

look _____ _____ _____

More verbs

The **tense** of a verb tells us whether something is happening now or whether it has happened already.

I **am eating** the cake.

This is the **present tense**.

I **ate** the cake.

This is the **past tense**.

I Underline the past tense verb in bold to complete each sentence.

a Rob **walks walked** home last night.

b Last year I **went goes** to France.

c My glass **is was** full before I drank my juice.

d Mum **fixed fixes** my bike this morning.

e Last Saturday we **bakes baked** a cake.

f Yesterday I **swaps swapped** a toy with Ben.

g Dad **drives drove** us to the party last Tuesday.

h Mum **hid hides** my presents before last Christmas.

i I **worry worried** before last week's test.

j Sally **tried tries** to catch the last bus yesterday.

II Complete this chart by filling in the missing past and present verbs.

Present	Past		Present	Past
a give	_____	g _____	copied
b _____	tapped	h wash	_____
c _____	skipped	i speak	_____
d mix	_____	j _____	built
e bring	_____	k am	_____
f _____	caught	l _____	grew

9

Question marks and exclamation marks

Not all sentences end with a full stop.

Question marks, ?, tell us someone is asking a question.

Exclamation marks, !, show a strong feeling like joy, anger or surprise.

Where are you**?**

Here I am**!**

I Draw lines to match up the two halves of each sentence. Make sure each completed sentence makes sense.

a Where is   hiss!

b The firework went   'Stop! Thief!'

c What time   my shoe?

d Who is   first prize!

e The policeman shouted,   bang!

f I won   does the bus go?

g Can I   knocking at the door?

h The angry snake went   go to Jo's house?

II Each of these sentences needs either a question mark or an exclamation mark. Fill in the correct one.

a When is your birthday____

b We lost the match____

c Where did Will go____

d Rachel shouted, 'That's mine____'

e Where are my shoes____

f Will it be sunny tomorrow____

g My holiday was amazing____

h Why did you choose blue____

i Sean yelled, 'Ouch____'

j The thunder went boom____

More about writing speech

When we write what someone says, we also need to write who is saying it.

We can say more about what the person is saying, like whether it is a question or a reply.

'My hat is blue,' **said Paul**.

'Where did you get it?' **asked Alex**.

'From the junkyard,' **replied Chris**.

I **Circle the name of the person speaking in each sentence. Then underline the word that tells us more about what they are saying.**

a 'Stop it!' <u>shouted</u> (Jack)

b 'Where is my book?' asked Sophie.

c 'It is on your bed,' answered Mum.

d 'Shall we go out?' suggested Tim.

e 'Good idea!' replied Ella.

f Jake grumbled, 'My head hurts.'

g Lucy asked, 'What time is it?'

h Dad explained, 'The toy is broken.'

i Sally demanded, 'Why can't I?'

j Mum replied, 'Because it is late.'

II **Underline the best word in bold to complete each sentence.**

a 'I am going out,' **said asked** James.

b 'Where are you going?' **explained asked** Chloe.

c 'I need to post a letter,' **demanded replied** James.

d 'Could you post one for me?' **questioned argued** Ryan.

e 'Of course,' **asked answered** James.

f 'It is to my friend Asher,' **requested explained** Ryan.

g 'It is raining,' **commented queried** Chloe.

h 'No it's not,' **questioned argued** James.

i 'It is!' **giggled shouted** Chloe angrily.

j 'I am going anyway,' **insisted asked** James.

Adjectives

Adjectives are words that **describe** people or things.

fluffy kitten

fast car

I **Underline the adjectives in these sentences.**

a The king was very old.

b I am reading a brilliant book.

c Claire was sleepy.

d The postman brought a square parcel.

e My brother is naughty.

f My new coat is blue.

g Dad wears green socks.

h It is a cold day today.

i The joke was funny.

j The teacher is angry.

II **Put these adjectives into their correct groups. Then add one example of your own.**

a huge

b frosty

c windy

d angry

e tiny

f rainy

g grumpy

h massive

i sunny

j friendly

k small

l cheerful

Adjectives describing the weather

_____

_____

_____

_____

_____

Adjectives describing size

_____

_____

_____

_____

_____

Adjectives describing moods

_____

_____

_____

_____

_____

Suffixes *er* and *est*

We can make adjectives **tell us more** about the person or thing they are describing by adding letters such as *er* or *est*.

These groups of letters are called suffixes.

a big present	a bigg**er** present	the bigg**est** present

I Fill in the gaps. Look carefully at how the spelling changes when you add *er* or *est*.

		Add *er*	Add *est*
a	quick	_____	quickest
b	long	longer	_____
c	nice	_____	nicest
d	_____	later	latest
e	hot	hotter	_____
f	fat	_____	fattest
g	_____	angrier	angriest

II Underline the *er* or *est* word in each sentence that is spelt wrong, then write it again correctly at the end.

a My jokes are much funnyer than Ben's, but Andy's are the funniest of all.

_____

b Ginny lives closer to the park than we do, but Sally lives the closeest of all.

_____

c I need a bigger pair of shoes, but even the bigest in the shop do not fit me.

_____

d Yesterday was sunier than Monday, but tomorrow is supposed to be the sunniest day so far this year.

_____

e I changed my picture to make the girl in it look happyer, but the boy has the happiest face.

_____

Singulars and plurals

One thing is known as the singular. **More than one** thing is a plural.

When you change from singular to plural, you need to know how to change the spelling. Most words add *s*.

cat

cats

Words ending with a hissing, buzzing or shushing sound end in *es*.

bush

bush**es**

Words ending in a consonant + *y* change the y to *ie*, then add *s*.

jelly

jell**ies**

I **Write down the plurals of these nouns.**

a shoe _____

b loss _____

c strawberry _____

d pony _____

e witch _____

f window _____

g cup _____

h baby _____

i city _____

j box _____

II **Choose the correct plural spelling from the words in bold to complete each sentence. Then write the correct word in the space.**

a Our dog has had nine _____. **puppys   puppies**

b We are going on holiday in eight _____. **dayes   days**

c In the woods, we saw a pheasant and two _____. **foxes   foxs**

d The fairy in the story granted the prince three _____. **wishes   wishs**

e There are two _____ in my village. **farmes   farms**

f There are seven _____ in our street. **houses   housies**

Silent letters

Some words contain letters that do not make a sound.

knight

rhino

These letters are silent.

I Underline the silent letters in these words.

a knee

b gnome

c write

d honest

e when

f thumb

g debt

h half

i folk

j should

II Circle the silent letter words in the wordsearch grid.

knot
gnu
wrinkle
sword
could
whale
chemist
lamb
doubt
yolk

c	f	q	r	t	w	y	u	i
a	s	t	d	f	h	c	t	o
s	c	s	v	l	a	m	b	p
w	r	i	n	k	l	e	u	l
o	c	m	r	u	e	c	o	c
r	c	e	l	g	c	c	d	c
d	c	h	j	n	k	n	o	t
q	p	c	o	u	l	d	t	y
a	b	z	w	i	o	f	j	j
m	n	b	v	x	y	b	z	a

Compound words

Compound words are made up of two smaller words.

 +  =

foot + ball = football

I **Write down the short words within these compound words.**

a _____ + _____ = dustbin

b _____ + _____ = popcorn

c _____ + _____ = doorstep

d _____ + _____ = playground

e _____ + _____ = cloakroom

f _____ + _____ = everyone

g _____ + _____ = clockwork

h _____ + _____ = cupboard

II **Look at the pictures. Then write out the word sums.**

a  _____ + _____ = _____

b  _____ + _____ = _____

c 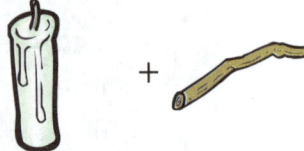 _____ + _____ = _____

d  _____ + _____ = _____

e _____ + _____ = _____

f  _____ + _____ = _____

cherry + s =

baby + s =

like + ing =

cup + s =

box + s =

fly + s =

laze + y =

watch + s =

key + s =

win + ing

make + ing

look + ing =

fat + est =

close + er =

big + er =

smell + y =

happy + est =

funny + er =

Adding to words

We can sometimes add **suffixes** to words to change their meaning.

care**ful**

care**less**

Look how *full* loses an *l* when it is used as a suffix.

Less does not lose an *s* when it is used as a suffix.

I **Complete these word sums. Remember that when you add *ful* or *less* to a word ending in *y*, you must change the *y* to *i*.**

a hope + ful = _____

b help + less = _____

c end + less = _____

d pity + ful = _____

e beauty + ful = _____

f thank + less = _____

g fear + less = _____

h home + less = _____

i forget + ful = _____

j mercy + ful = _____

II **Write a sentence using each of these words.**

a painful _____

b speechless _____

c successful _____

d jobless _____

e wishful _____

f penniless _____

g joyful _____

h friendless _____

17

Joining words together

When two words are often used together, we can sometimes join them by taking out some letters and using an apostrophe.

I **am** long.

I'm even longer.

This is an apostrophe, **'**. It replaces the letter *a* in **I am**.

I Draw lines to match the pairs of words with their shortened forms.

a should not   don't

b she will   I'll

c there is   shouldn't

d is not   I've

e I will   she'll

f do not   wouldn't

g it is   it's

h would not   there's

i I have   isn't

II Write down the shortened versions of these words.

a I would   _____

b does not _____

c will not   _____

d I had   _____

e she is   _____

f he has   _____

g they would_____

h where is   _____

i who is   _____

j have not   _____

Alphabetical order

If a list of words all start with the same letter, we can use the next letter to put them in alphabetical order.

b<u>a</u>ll

b<u>e</u>d

a comes before **e** in the alphabet, so **ball** comes before **bed**.

 I Write these names again in alphabetical order.

a Arthur   **e** Ashley   1 _____   5 _____

b Abigail   **f** Amy   2 _____   6 _____

c Anthony   **g** Aiden   3 _____   7 _____

d Alice   **h** Attia   4 _____   8 _____

II Look at the first two letters of each animal to help you find them in the alphabetical index of this book. Then write down the page number.

a bats _____

b birds _____

c chickens _____

d ducks _____

e cows _____

f bees _____

g cats _____

h deer _____

i crows _____

j dogs _____

Animals	Page Number
	55
bats	12
bees	18
birds	50
cats	33
chickens	29
cows	82
crows	46
deer	6
dogs	63
ducks	

Opposites

Words with opposite meanings are called **antonyms**.

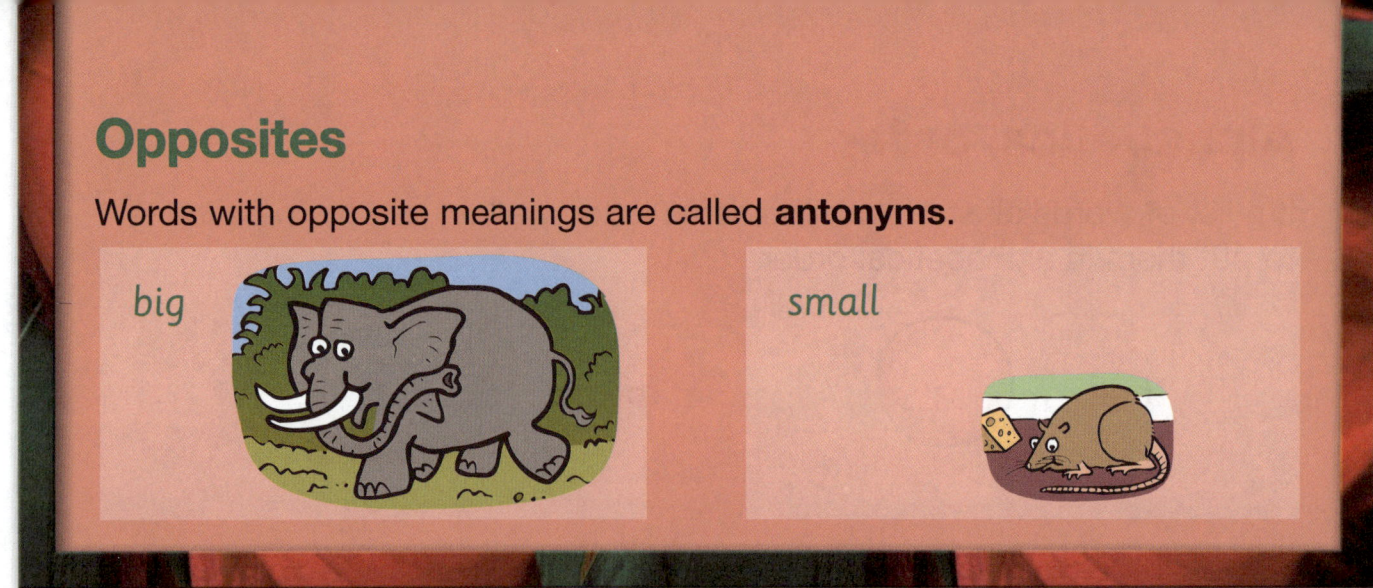

big   small

I Draw lines to match up the antonyms.

a true	disagree
b happy	fast
c fat	low
d heavy	new
e dry	unfair
f slow	light
g high	thin
h old	unhappy
i agree	wet
j fair	false

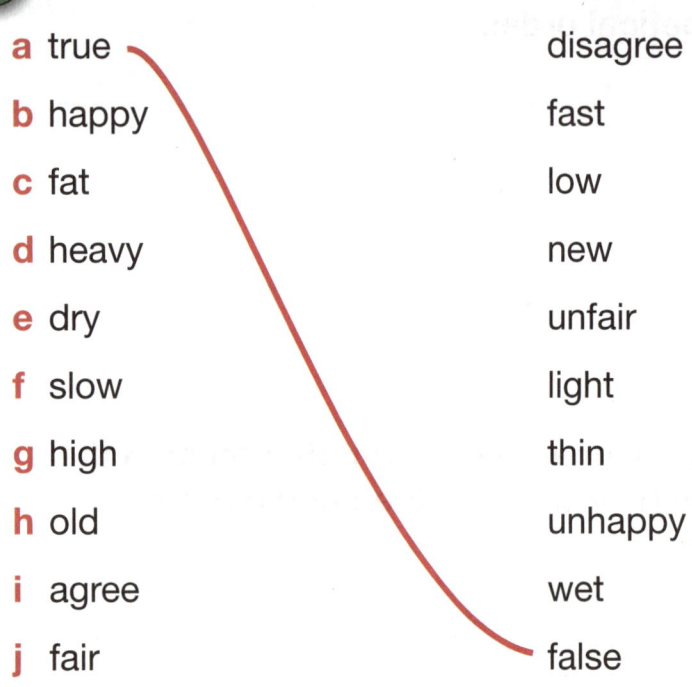

II Write down antonyms for these words.

a night _____   **i** short _____

b polite _____   **j** obey _____

c fast _____   **k** pretty _____

d right _____   **l** asleep _____

e helpful _____

f honest _____

g upstairs _____

h kind _____

Pronouns

Pronouns can sometimes be used instead of nouns.

> Tom likes **dogs**.   dogs = noun
>
> Tom likes **them**.   them = pronoun

When you are talking about yourself, you use **I, me** or **my**. These are all pronouns.

> I like my dinner.
>
> Aaron plays with me.

I Underline the pronouns in these sentences. Look carefully as some sentences contain more than one!

a I ate my lunch.

b Will you be at school?

c I went to his party.

d Ali walked with them.

e We are going fishing.

f Ruby is my best friend.

g This game is mine.

h I played with her.

i Pete walks his dog.

j The boys did their homework.

II Rewrite these sentences, replacing the bold nouns with a pronoun from the brackets.

a Emma opened **Emma's** presents. (**his her their**)

_____

b **The boys** gobbled their sandwiches. (**We They You**)

_____

c **Lucy** is my cousin. (**He She It**)

_____

d **My teacher and I** tidied the classroom. (**We I They**)

_____

e The king sat on **the king's** throne. (**my their his**)

_____

f **Mum and Dad** are going out tonight. (**We They You**)

_____

Collective nouns

Collective nouns describe **groups of things**.

A **herd** of elephants

A **pack** of wolves

These are collective nouns.

I Pick a word from the box to complete these collective nouns.

a a flock of _____

b a swarm of _____

c a flight of _____

d a deck of _____

e a bunch of _____

f a litter of _____

g a pride of _____

h a gaggle of _____

i a troupe of _____

j a shoal of _____

cards
fish
sheep
monkeys
geese
stairs
bees
lions
puppies
flowers

II Think of your own collective nouns for these things.

a a _____ of horses

b a _____ of books

c a _____ of cars

d a _____ of frogs

e a _____ of bears

f a _____ of ducks

Commas

Commas tell readers when to **pause**.

Paul had tea, then he went home.

They also separate items in a **list**.

We bought apples, bananas, grapes and pears.

I Look carefully at the commas in these sentences. Circle the commas in lists. Underline the commas used to show a pause.

a Joe, my brother, is eight years old.

b For lunch, we had sausages, chips, peas and carrots.

c I'm wearing trousers, a shirt, socks and shoes.

d Actually, it is quite warm today.

e The bag split, so the shopping went everywhere.

f In stories, the knight always kills the dragon.

g You need sugar, flour, eggs and butter to bake a cake.

h Anyway, it was all fine in the end.

II Add commas to these sentences. Read the words out loud to help you decide where the pauses or lists are.

a Mrs Smith my teacher marked my work.

b My best friends are Chris Sam and Jo.

c In the end I chose the blue coat.

d Although it was late we played one more game.

e Last night after Dad came home we watched TV.

f Alex my best friend lives next door.

g At the zoo we saw elephants lions camels and giraffes.

h Eventually I found the missing book.

Capital letters

We use capital letters at the start of sentences. They are also used for special names, like the names of people and places, days of the week or months.

On Sunday, I am going to London with Sarah.

I **Circle the letters that should be in capitals.**

a tomorrow is saturday.

b my dog is called toby.

c i cannot wait for christmas.

d gran lives in manchester.

e dr smith took my temperature.

f mum is painting my bedroom.

g my brother is called steven.

h yesterday mum took us to bristol zoo.

II **Write this passage again, adding the capital letters.**

my dog is called toby. we bought him in march from a man called mr havers who lives in barn lane. he was my birthday present so i got to choose him.

_____

_____

_____

_____

_____

_____

Writing instructions

Written instructions tell us how to do something.

> To get to my house, turn right at the school gates. Then, turn left at the roundabout. I live at number 32.

Good instructions give us the important information in the right order.

I **These instructions for making a banana smoothie are muddled up. Put them in the right order by numbering them 1–6.**

a _____ Serve immediately.

b _____ Place banana in a blender with milk.

c _____ Pour into a chilled glass.

d _____ Ask an adult to blend the ingredients until smooth.

e _____ Peel one banana.

f _____ Add one scoop of vanilla ice cream.

II **These sentences are instructions, but they are all muddled up. Write the sentences in the right order.**

Use your finger or a pencil to make a hole about 3 cm deep. Cover with soil. Keep soil just damp until seedling appears. Fill the pot with soil, leaving a gap at the top. Drop a sunflower seed into the hole. Find a small flower pot.

a _____

b _____

c _____

d _____

e _____

f _____

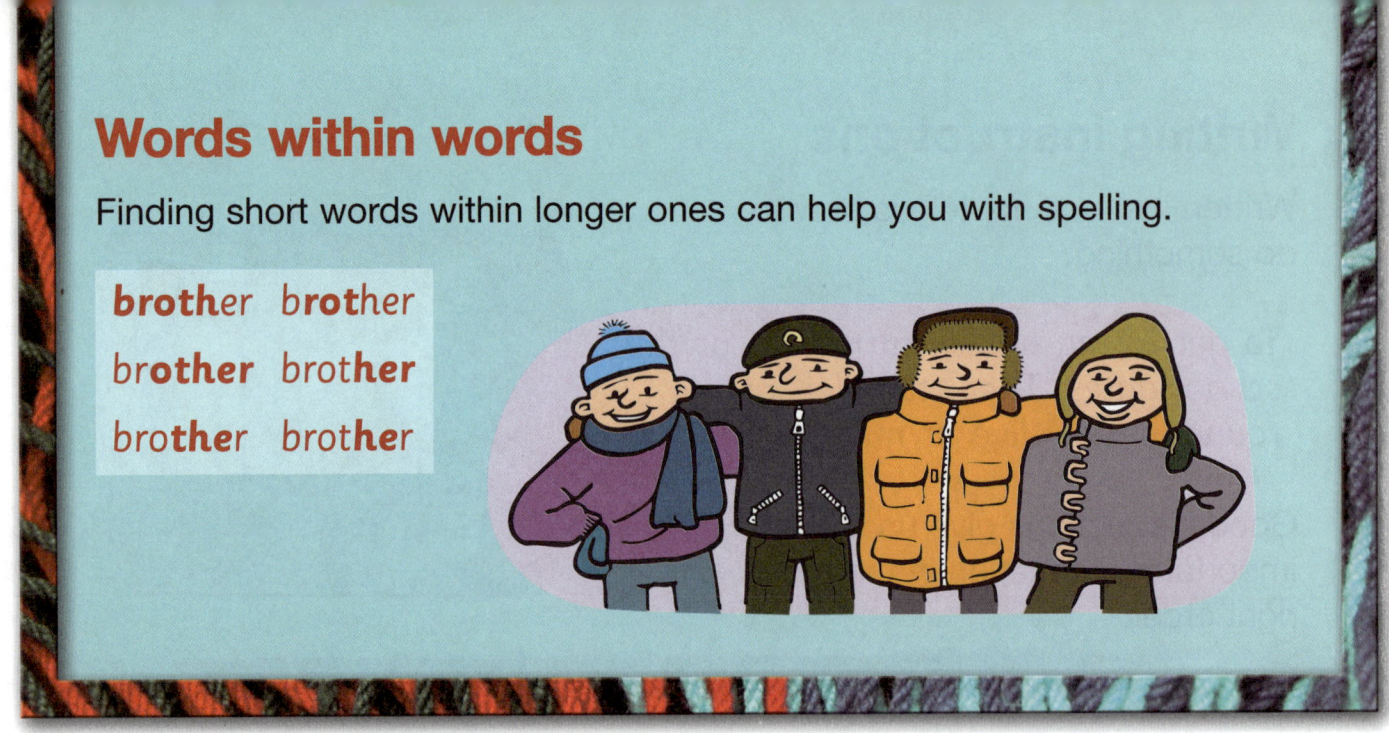

Words within words

Finding short words within longer ones can help you with spelling.

broth**er**   **br**ot**her**
brother   **br**ot**her**
brother   **br**ot**her**

I Draw lines to match up each long word with the short one within it.

a never   ear

b what   air

c hand   one

d bear   ever

e stairs   late

f pillow   rage

g plate   cream

h garage   hat

i bone   low

j scream   and

II Write down two short words within each of the longer ones.

a stable   _____ _____

b another _____ _____

c pretend _____ _____

d forest   _____ _____

e further _____ _____

f them   _____ _____

g where   _____ _____

h shelf   _____ _____

i wheel   _____ _____

j shame   _____ _____

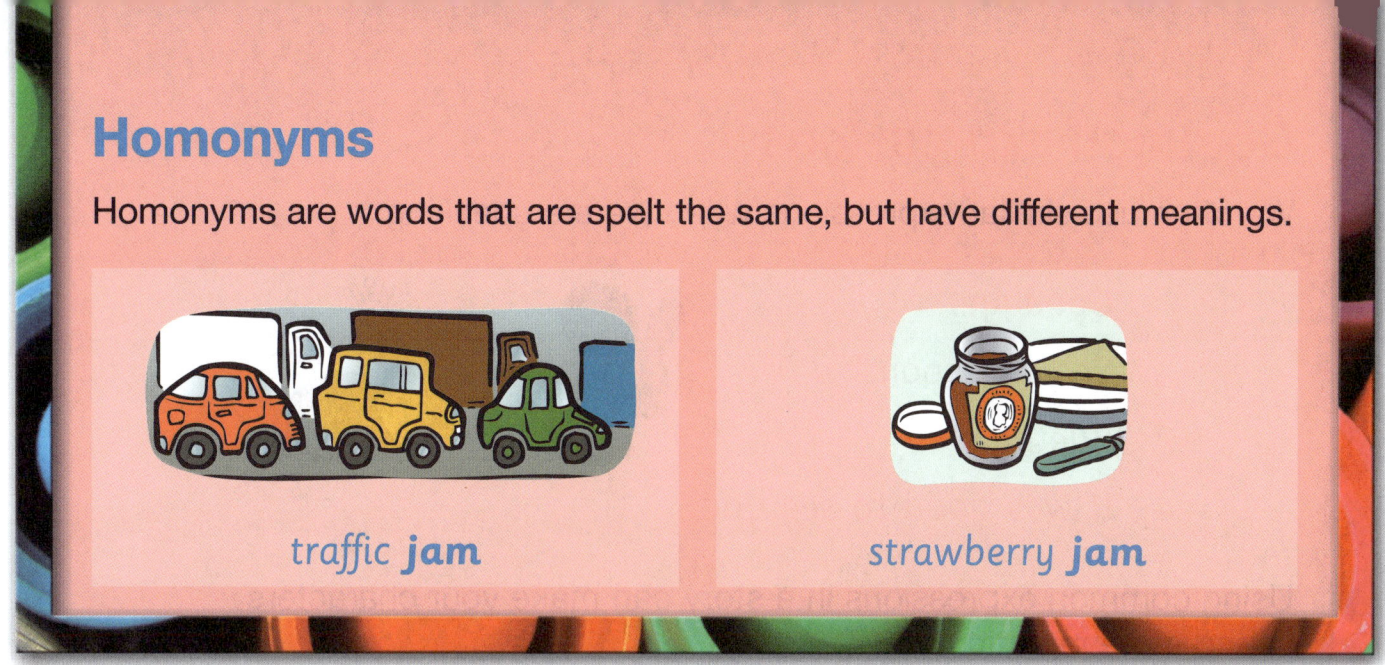

Homonyms

Homonyms are words that are spelt the same, but have different meanings.

traffic **jam**

strawberry **jam**

I Circle the words in this group that have homonyms.

hair	fit	sky	lamp
plain	bear	door	wave
cat	bat	lead	pear
watch	hat	rose	band

II Write two sentences for each word showing two different meanings.

a form

_____

_____

b bank

_____

_____

c ring

_____

_____

d light

_____

_____

Common expressions

We often use similar expressions when we are speaking.

> 'Goodbye.'
>
> 'See you soon.'
>
> 'Bye bye.'
>
> 'It was good to see you.'

Using common expressions in a story can make your characters sound more realistic.

I **Sort these expressions into groups on the chart.**

a I'm sorry

b Thank you!

c I don't believe it!

d Forgive me

e Cheer up

f Please excuse me

g Wow!

h Thanks

i That's amazing!

j Chin up

k Don't worry

l You're so kind

Expressions of thanks	Expressions of apology	Expressions of comfort	Expressions of surprise
_____	_____	_____	_____
_____	_____	_____	_____
_____	_____	_____	_____

II **Fill in three more expressions for each group in the table.**

Expressions of warning

_____Look out!_____

_____

_____

Expressions of greeting

_____Hello_____

_____

_____

_____

More singulars and plurals

When we change from singular to plural, sometimes the spellings change and sometimes the whole word changes. Sometimes the word stays exactly the same.

Singular	Plural
He eats the cake.	**They** eat the cakes.

pronoun   verb   noun

pronoun: the whole word has changed

verb and noun: the spellings have changed

I Fill in all the plurals. The first one has been done for you.

Singular	Plural		Singular	Plural
he runs	they run		I walk	_____
she swims	_____		I eat	_____
I laugh	_____		she pushes	_____
he sleeps	_____		he wishes	_____
she builds	_____		I hope	_____

II Write these sentences again in the plural, making sure the nouns, verbs and pronouns are all plural.

a She picks the flower.

_____

b He kicks the ball.

_____

c I sharpen the pencil.

_____

d She washes the car.

_____

Conjunctions

Conjunctions are words that can **join** two short sentences together.

> I took my umbrella.
> It was raining.
>
> I took my umbrella,
> **because** it was raining.

 **Underline the conjunctions in these sentences.**

a I turned the TV on when my favourite programme started.

b I did my homework, so I could go and play.

c I called for Asif, but he was out.

d Kelly likes bananas, but I like apples.

e I went to bed, because I was tired.

f I stayed at home, while Mum went shopping.

g Drew was just leaving when we arrived.

h I could wear my jeans or I could wear a skirt.

 **Choose a conjunction from the box to make the two short sentences into one sentence and rewrite the new sentence.**

a I got a drink. I was thirsty.

_____

b Chris wants a skateboard. Mum said no.

_____

c Luke was three. I was born.

_____

d We waited. Dad packed up the car.

_____

e I could go bowling. I could go swimming.

_____

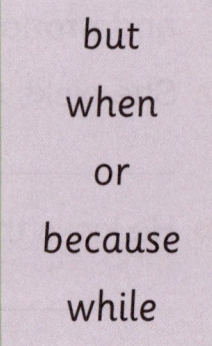

but
when
or
because
while

First and third person accounts

If I write about what I am doing, this is called a **first person** account.

I kicked the ball.

If I write about what someone else does,
this is called a **third person** account.

Ella kicked the ball.

I Read these sentences, then decide whether each one is a first person or third person account. Tick the right box.

	First person	Third person
a Sean lost his bag.	☐	☐
b I had chicken pox.	☐	☐
c My cat is called Monty.	☐	☐
d They went to America on holiday.	☐	☐
e Dad missed the train.	☐	☐
f I live in a town.	☐	☐
g Lee and Kerry played football.	☐	☐
h I walk to school.	☐	☐

II Read this third person account of life in the Handy family. Imagine you are Sarah Handy and rewrite it as a first person account.

The Handy family live in a small house in Bridge Street. They have a dog and a cat. Sarah Handy plays netball and is learning to play the violin. Her best friend is called Leah.

_____

_____

_____

_____

_____

ANSWERS

Page 2

I ight light, fright, bright
oa boat, goat, loan
ame name, frame, tame
ay play, hay, lay

II Many answers are possible.

Page 3

I a hoping
b baking
c clapping
d spinning
e winning
f losing
g shutting
h fitting
i making
j swimming
k slipping

II a riding
b planning
c sitting
d shopping
e staring
f jogging
g slipping
h hating
i rubbing
j hitting
k raising
l shaking

Page 4

I a apple
b metal
c parcel
d channel
e double
f ripple
g label
h pedal
i cannibal
j puddle

II a model
b kettle
c medical
d bicycle
e panel
f travel
g little
h table

Page 5

I a unable
b unseen
c disqualify
d unusual
e disobey
f unpopular
g undo
h disappear
i disown
j untidy

II un unwell, unkind, unlucky
dis disallow, disagree, dishonest
re recycle, return, rebuild
pre prepare, predict, previous,

Page 6

I a huge, large
b tiny, small
c excellent, brilliant
d freezing, chilly
e unkind, mean
f after, later
g glum, unhappy
h pleased, joyful

II Many answers are possible.

Page 7

I a 'My best friend is Max,' said Joel.
b 'I love football,' said Rita.
c 'We are going swimming today,' said Mum.
d Martin said, 'That is my bag.'
e 'I have a new puppy,' said Alfie.

f The teacher said, 'It is raining today.'
g Dad shouted, 'Do not forget your coat!'
h 'Let us watch TV,' said Sophie.

II a 'I am going skating tomorrow,' said Heather.
b Sarah said, 'That is not fair!'
c Harry sighed, 'I love chocolate cake!'
d 'I would like a drink please,' said Lucy.
e 'Look at my new bike,' said Katy.
f The bus driver called out, 'This is your stop.'
g 'Time to tidy up,' shouted Mrs Moors.
h Gran said, 'See you soon!'

Page 8

I a shines
b fly
c reads
d paints
e watches
f waits
g munches
h turn
i shut
j rings

II run dash, sprint, jog
make build, create, assemble
sleep slumber, snooze, doze
look see, peer, watch

Page 9

I a walked
b went
c was
d fixed
e baked
f swapped
g drove
h hid
i worried
j tried

II a gave
b tap
c skip
d mixed
e brought
f catch
g copy
h washed
i spoke
j build
k was
l grow

Page 10

I a Where is my shoe?
b The firework went bang!
c What time does the bus go?
d Who is knocking at the door?
e The policeman shouted, 'Stop! Thief!'
f I won first prize!
g Can I go to Jo's house?
h The angry snake went hiss!

II Sentences needing question marks: a, c, e, f, h
Sentences needing exclamation marks: b, d, g, i, j

Page 11

I a 'Stop it!' shouted Jack.
b 'Where is my book?' asked Sophie.
c 'It is on your bed,' answered Mum.
d 'Shall we go out?' suggested Tim.
e 'Good idea!' replied Ella.
f Jake grumbled, 'My head hurts.'
g Lucy asked, 'What time is it?'
h Dad explained, 'The toy is broken.'
i Sally demanded, 'Why can't I?'
j Mum replied, 'Because it is late.'

II a said
b asked
c replied
d questioned
e answered
f explained
g commented
h argued
i shouted
j insisted

Page 12

I a old
b brilliant
c sleepy
d square
e naughty
f blue
g green
h cold
i funny
j angry

II Adjectives describing the weather: frosty, windy, rainy, sunny
Adjectives describing size: huge, tiny, massive, small
Adjectives describing moods: angry, grumpy, friendly, cheerful
Check child's examples.

Page 13

I a quicker
b longest
c nicer
d late
e hottest
f fatter
g angry

II a funnier
b closest
c biggest
d sunnier
e happier

Page 14

I a shoes
b losses
c strawberries
d ponies
e witches
f windows
g cups
h babies
i cities
j boxes

II a puppies
b days
c foxes
d wishes
e farms
f houses

Page 15

I a knee
b gnome
c write
d honest
e when
f thumb
g debt
h half
i folk
j should